MW01268184

Forgiving
the Unforgettable

By

Cordie Daniels

Hairstylist/Makeup Artist: Steven P. Daniels.
Photographers: Lisa Courts (front cover)
Eric Arnold (Back cover)

Editor: Shari Armstrong
Interior Layout: Tony Bradford
ISBN 978-1-938950-53-7

Greater Is He Publishing
9824 E. Washington St.
Chagrin Falls, Ohio 44023
Phone: 216.288.9315
www.GreaterIsHePublishing.com

CONTENTS

Acknowledgments

Thank You

"In every thing give thanks: for this is the will of God in Christ Jesus concerning you." (1 Thessalonians 5:18, King James Version)

Throughout my journey, I am grateful for the people that God has placed in my life. Lord, I thank you for your mercy, grace, and deliverance concerning my story. Thank you for choosing me to be used for your glory. I didn't recognize your presence then; however, I now see your hand of protection was with me at all times. You are so faithful. My life journey has been to be a testimony to help others.

I thank you with all my heart and soul for my parents; may they rest in peace knowing their wrong decisions did not destroy me. I now understand they loved me with all of the understanding of love they had.

Thank you for my loving friend and soul mate, Hairstylist/Makeup Artist Steven P. Daniels. You equipped him with what I needed in a husband. Thank you for my three children, Steven II, Brandon, and Mikaela, who truly hold the keys to my heart. I release them back to you to be used for your glory. Mommy loves you with all of my heart.

A very special appreciation to Missionary Clarine "Big Ma" Heffner for opening your doors to a troubled teen. Your words of encouragement, teachings, and taking me to church introduced me to Christ. I love you dearly.

1

To Elder and Mother "Madea" Hall. You answered the call and imparted your wisdom and knowledge in me. Your example of a Godly marriage and foundational teaching always taught me to focus on Christ. It is sustaining me while you are in glory. I will always love you both.

Elder James "Judah" and Alberta Patterson, your words of prophecy spoke life into me which caused this book to manifest. Your marital advice is so greatly appreciated.

Thank you to all the many others who have blessed me; thank you. I am so grateful. May God bless you all.

Cordie Buttrom Daniels: Born in Buffalo, NY; Lover of Jesus Christ; Wife for 18 years; Mother; Sister of 11 half brothers & sisters; and Registered Nurse.

"Cordie Daniels is a woman of faith, strength and character whose sincere desire is to provide her family with all the pleasant memories she was not privy to as a child.

Although her childhood may have been filled with pain and abuse, she has prevailed to become a beacon of light that symbolizes triumph! She has a heart of a child and children adore her, MY children especially."

~Sondra M. Douglas, Esquire

"Cordie Daniels' story ~ one of faith, strength and resilience. She openly shares from her heart, revealing her personal disappointment, failure, faults and brokenness.

More importantly, Cordie gives her testimony, which speaks of God's power to not only mend broken hearts, but to totally restore, rebuild and transform lives. We published a short article about Cordie's story in REWIND, a quarterly magazine designed to build and strengthen marriages God's way. Immediately, we received numerous responses about how her story ministered to our readers. We know her full story will minister to everyone who reads it as well."

~Terrance and Tamara Hundley,
Publishers of REWIND Magazine
www.rewindmarriage.com

"This book will bring healing to your life. As you read it, open your heart to forgiveness. Congrats to Cordie for a job well done. God be praised. Share it with a loved one and friend."

~Elder James (Judah) Patterson.

My Story

Although Satan had the go ahead to hit me from every angle and plans to allow generational curses to destroy my life, he failed. After accepting Christ in my life, I had such a determination and passion for life that I took my childhood anger and turned it into positive energy that motivated me to allow God to use my testimony to help others. I no longer took life struggles and disappointment personally, but as my purpose.

I know that it is because of God that I have a heart and passion for people who are hurting. I want my testimony to be used to encourage those people who feel like giving up in life, unworthy, ugly, dumb, or have no purpose in life; to make sure they know that with Christ, their life can be so much better. He will show you the whys and show you how those life struggles have even worked out in your favor, making those dreams in your life come true.

I remember some happy days with just my mom and brothers living in the apartment, alone, after she left her previous relationship with a deaf mute man. We never learned how to communicate with him. He threw my mother from a second or third story window. One day, I saw him hitting my mother, so I went into the kitchen and grabbed a heavy, black pan that my mom used to bake cornbread in. I lifted it in the air to hit him with it in the back of the head. His friend stopped me, allowing him to continue to hit my mom. But after she left him, I was very happy and felt my mom was safe. If I had experienced such a relationship, I would have become a nun, but not my mom. She was a tough little fireball, with a lot of mouth.

The best times were when my mother would be sober. She was the first one to take me to church. As a little girl, I would climb in bed with her, minus the boyfriend. We would just cuddle and talk until we fell asleep. When she would get the welfare money for us, we would walk to the Goodwill and she would shop for clothes for us, and I would shop for clothes for my baby dolls. I love to do that now with my daughter. Those checks came twice a month, and she would always buy a pizza, which was a treat. Before her boyfriend, my mom loved to dance and laugh at my brothers and my jokes. After she would straighten my hair with the hot comb, I would be crying because of the pain. She would grab my face, kiss me and say, "Momma's sorry, baby." That would take the pain away.

One Christmas, when it was just my mom, brothers and me living alone, we had a lot of toys under the tree. She did love us, and when sober and man-less, she really tried to raise us the best she could. However, when a boyfriend entered the picture, our welfare money would be gone after only one day. We lived off of German bologna sandwiches, except for holidays. My mom was a very good cook, and on holidays, she would cook a big meal for us.

But we still had times when we had no toothpaste, deodorant, and no toilet tissue and had to use newspaper.

But on Christmases when there was a boyfriend, we just got one toy per person. One time, I got Play-Doh, and my mom looked so sad giving it to me. I lied to my friends about what I got for Christmas that year. Another Christmas, my mom had me lie to her boyfriend about her whereabouts because he always had to know her every move. When I got up to look for gifts under the tree, I was met by her boyfriend telling me that he knew I had lied. I knew not to tell him that I was just telling him what my mom said to say, because he would have hit her. I just stayed quiet and looked at my mom. The next thing I knew, this giant slapped me so hard, with a hand larger than my face, it made my whole body turn. My Coca-Cola glasses went flying down to the end of the hallway. My mom knew I lied for her. She came in my room and saw I was crying, gave me a hug and promised to buy me some candy. I never got that candy.

It was the alcohol, drugs, and men that took her away from me. I may not be able to think of a lot of wise phrases she told me, or things that she should have told me to stay away from, or a lot of things I should have been taught as I was growing up into a young lady. A lot of my street smarts came from being out there and learning all her what-not-to-dos.

Beginning of Trust Betrayed

(Warning: Graphic Content)

I was five years old when the sexual abuse began. I can remember it as if it were yesterday. It was a sunny day in the projects. The bed was positioned horizontally across the window, allowing the sunrays in, giving the room warmth, but it still had a cold feel. My mother had left us home with a neighbor's teenage son, or he may have been around twenty, while she went grocery shopping. I knew him very well because he lived in an apartment downstairs with his mom. She was a very good friend of my mom's that I called auntie, because close friends of your parents were often called auntie and uncle. He was like an older cousin. I remember the trust and love that I had in this family friend. He was always extra nice to me, playing with me as if I was his little sister. He always gave me a big smile when I saw him.

My memory is a blank on how he actually got me alone in the room. Because of the trust I placed in him, I'm sure all he did was ask me to come in. My next memory is of him sitting on the foot of the bed with his back to the door as if he was enjoying the sunrays. He was so tall that if my brothers were to walk by, they would not have been able to see me or know what was going on. His pants were still up, but his penis was in my mouth. My stomach knots up as I remember it and type about it. Chills run down my spine. And yet, even with my maturity, I understand why the little girl in me still cries out, "Why would he betray my trust in him?" But, because of Christ in me, I am able to live in forgiveness.

THEREFORE IF ANY MAN BE IN CHRIST, HE IS A NEW CREATURE: OLD THINGS ARE PASSED AWAY; BEHOLD, ALL THINGS ARE BECOME NEW. (2 Corinthians 5:17, King James Version)

I was scared, but at the same time I wasn't because of the trust I had in him. I trusted that he wouldn't hurt me, so what he was asking me to do must be okay, even though I didn't like it nor understand it. I didn't even give it a second thought. Wow! Trust is very powerful. It's almost like faith. Now, if we as adults could have that much faith in God: "

If only we as adults had this childlike faith in God, we would not have to go through nearly half of the trials we encounter because we would just do what our creator says.

> **AND SAID, VERILY I SAY UNTO YOU, EXCEPT YE BE CONVERTED, AND BECOME AS LITTLE CHILDREN, YE SHALL NOT ENTER INTO THE KINGDOM OF HEAVEN. (Matthew 18:3, King James Version)**

I remember the feeling of being paralyzed with the pressure of trying to please him because in my eyes, he was like a nice, big brother--not understanding why he was controlling my head, making it go in an up and down motion. He allowed it until my mouth began to fill with what I thought at the time to be pee. I at least knew that pee-pee belonged in the toilet. Not wanting to swallow, I tried to lift my head, but I was met with resistance from a large hand that was stronger than me. I remember my eyes widened as fear overtook me, and thinking during the struggle, "Why is he peeing in my mouth?" After he stopped holding my head down, I was released. I got up, horrified and very confused, and ran to the bathroom. I don't even remember crying, just that I could not stop washing my mouth out enough, trying to relieve myself of feeling dirty.

In my mind, I could not figure out who was in the wrong, not ever being taught what to do when someone does a bad touch to you. I didn't know what to do. So just going on my experience of being called stupid, dumb, and many other names that I as an adult don't say, I came to the conclusion that I must be to blame. I must have done something to make this person who was always nice to me want to put what I

9

thought was pee in my mouth. I'd better not tell anyone because I will be the one blamed. Filled with guilt, I erased it from my mind. He eventually left his mom's house to go live with someone else, so I never saw him again. I only saw his mother and other siblings; he was out of sight, out of mind. I never ever told anyone, not my mother nor any friends, because I felt embarrassed and dirty.

Life with the Devil

The safe environment only lasted a short time before my mom had a new boyfriend, Lucifer in the flesh. It would be the beginning of literally living in hell, fearful of being killed by him from the age of six until I was in the 10th grade. I have to admit, if my mom didn't teach me anything about men, she definitely taught me who not to pick. I can spot an abuser a mile away.

This all led to the beginning of my low self-esteem. I was about seven years old by now, thinking I must be this bad little girl to have made this nice person want to do what I now knew was a bad thing to me. I must have asked for it, but still I knew in my soul I would never have done it. I just couldn't remember how he got me to do such a thing. But, being the only girl living with three brothers, I often felt lonely and left out, so I was taken by anybody who would give me attention.

The first time my mom brought Lucifer home, it was at night and my brothers and I were home alone. I was sleeping on the couch. I woke up in this stranger's arms, scared and confused, with my mom standing next to him with a big smile on her face. She was trying to reassure me that it was okay. Even though I didn't like seeing another man in our home, I allowed him to carry me to my bed.

He moved in right away, acting nice; as months went on, his demons could no longer hide their faces. His anger and rage became very vivid. He started trying to destroy whatever brought my mom happiness. My mom brought home a stray kitten because she loved animals. He came home drunk, like he often did. My brothers and I all knew to stay out of sight, but poor Kitty didn't know that.

Kitty walked within arm's reach of him while he was slumped over on the couch. For no reason, he picked her up. I heard him cursing at her, so I ran to get her. But, as I got to the living room, I saw him throw Kitty like a dodge ball against the refrigerator. I was sure she was dead after sliding down the front of the refrigerator. She was lying still on the floor, not making a sound. My brothers and I cried as we watched him pick her up and toss her lifeless little body in the dumpster.

When our mom got home, Lucifer was asleep. We told her what happened to Kitty. I could tell my mom was very upset and hurt, but afraid to say anything to him. She told my brother and me to come with her so we could get Kitty and bury her. As we got closer to the dumpster, to our surprise, we heard a low whimpering and crying. My mom climbed in there and brought Kitty out. We took her into the house, and with Lucifer still asleep, she began nursing the kitten back to health.

She told us that some of her legs were broken, but she wasn't sure if all four were or not. She taped Popsicle sticks to all four of her legs. Within a couple of days, all you could hear was the clicking of the sticks hitting the floor as Kitty began to get her strength again and was running around. Mom did a great job of nursing her back to health. Lucifer didn't even remember what he had done, and we never spoke of it again. We just kept Kitty out of his sight.

Mom's friends that used to come over to our house were no longer welcome. One time, my mom's good friend came over who was living an open homosexual life. He was younger than her but older than us, and he used to call my mom "Momma." We all loved him, but Lucifer came home to find them drinking and smoking reefer. He told him to leave and never come back. Mom's young friend stated that he had the right to continue coming to our house as long as Momma invited him. He was not going to stay away because they had been friends for many years before Lucifer was even in the picture.

I was in my bedroom with the door closed, shaking and too scared to come out. I heard the loud cursing and arguing. I could hear my mom telling her friend to leave as Lucifer began to make threats because my mom knew he would carry them out. I guess the reefer and alcohol had our short and very skinny friend feeling like he was David. This six feet Goliath was no match for him, because he would not shut up nor leave. I began hearing my mom screaming, "No!" and David screaming. Lucifer stabbed him several times, and he received over fifty stitches. Thank God he lived. He refused to press charges and remained friends with us, but he only came over after Lucifer left to go to the bar.

My mother lost a lot more friends and family members, who stopped coming over. Lucifer now had complete control. The beatings on my mom always happened while we were in school or asleep. They would leave her with black eyes, and they became more and more frequent. My brothers and I were young and scared, but she did not let us call the police. She didn't like it when we told her to leave him. She would tell us that it was her life, and if we pushed, she would get angry with us.

I was always asking if I could stay the night over other people's houses. I was always trying to escape home. A lot of times, I was allowed to stay over a friend's house. Often, my friend's mom was a single, young parent, who would stay out all night, or not even come back home for two days. We would be there alone, usually caring for younger siblings. While I was seeking refuge, my friends were seeking security. They were afraid to stay home alone and needed help with the younger siblings as well. I was always the oldest among my friends.

Sometimes, Lucifer would leave me home alone and take my brother with him across town to the bar. He would often sneak him alcoholic drinks. One day, while still in elementary school, my brother got in a lot of trouble for telling his teacher she could not tell him what to do because he drinks liquor, smokes reefer, and he likes women.

Lucifer controlled the money so much that if I asked my mom for a quarter, she would tell me to ask him. I would only ask him if he was sober because sometimes he would be nice to me if he was. But, in order to get the quarter, I would have to give him a kiss on the lips in front of my mom. I would want to gag as my lips approached his discolored lips, due to pigmentation changes from years and years of alcohol abuse. There were no teeth behind them; he was all gums. My gag reflex is still kicking in as I type this.

Talk about kissing the enemy. The things I did for penny candy.

One night, he beat mom so badly that after she fell asleep, I called the paramedics. When they came, she lied about what happened as I watched them roll her out on a stretcher. I stood there as fear overtook me as reality began to set in. I was left with a monster that had made it very clear to my mom and me that he hated me. He had even threatened to kill me. For some reason, I felt in my soul that I was next because he was drunk. To this day, I cannot understand why she would leave me with him, knowing the true reason for her illness, why the paramedics didn't pick up on it, or why I didn't speak up.

Shortly after they left, he woke up to realize my mom was gone. My brother and I told him that she went to the hospital. He became very upset, especially when he learned she would be staying overnight. For some reason, I can't remember why, he hit me. I am sure I was not talking back to him because I was scared to death of him. I just remember we were standing outside of my bedroom door when he hit me in the face. I saw white stars. He began hitting me with his belt, over and over. I could see my brother watching, but he was too small to help. I could see that he felt very sad for me. When Lucifer saw my brother watching, he asked him if he should stop hitting me. Thank God my brother said yes. He still left me with a black eye.

Once my mom returned from the hospital, she noticed my eye and mentioned it to him. She hugged me, but nothing else was done about it. This must have happened in the summertime because I don't remember any teachers getting involved. I often thought about telling the police, but I was scared to leave my mom with him. I knew CPS would take me and that she would not leave him. I stayed because of her.

By this time, my self-esteem was zero. Death looked like a better option at times. I was always so afraid of being hit by anyone. I would avoid our little play area in the projects because the other kids would sense my fear and want to pick a fight. I found peace in being alone, and I still do. We would move from project to project often. We were living off the welfare system my mom received to care for her four kids as a single parent. Lucifer never had a job; however, on the 1st or 16th of the month, my mom would give him her whole check. He had her convinced that she was too dumb and incompetent to handle the bills on her own. I believe that she did it because she longed for a man to take care of her. For him, it just fed into his need for control and to feel like a man. Talk about being brainwashed. They were both codependent on each other in a negative way.

When You Put Your Trust in Man

My brothers and I all had different fathers. One day, one of my brothers was picked up by his father to sleep over at his house. Because my father was not in my life at this time, and my mom's live-in boyfriend hated me, I asked if I could go with my brother for a sleepover. His dad was always nice to me, but I didn't know him well. But any night away from my house was considered a safe night to me, getting away from my hater. He wasn't active in my brothers' life, but his being nice to me made me trust him.

This night continued to feed into my thoughts of being this bad little girl, someone who makes nice people do bad things to me for some reason. It started simply with him picking me up with a big smile on my face. For once, I felt so special, and I had someone's attention. That led to him picking me up from behind and having me sit on his lap while we were in the kitchen. He put his thumbs behind each of my armpits, with his other fingers resting on my very underdeveloped breasts. I mean, there wasn't even enough tissue in them to distinguish me from my brothers.

17

I became paralyzed as I felt his fingers begin to massage my chest. I remember sitting there, scared with a blank stare, watching my brother playing right in front of us, not knowing what was happening to me. I remember getting off his lap, acting as if I was clueless as to what had just happened, but knowing it was wrong. I stood in the bathroom, looking in the mirror, feeling guilty and not liking the little girl I saw in the mirror. I knew that I could not tell anyone because they would just believe that it was all my fault. I must have in some way asked for it. After all, I make nice people want to do bad things to me.

We were soon introduced to our "new uncle," who just happened to be a friend of Lucifer's that he made while in jail. I have many memories of staying overnight at his house with his wife and two step-daughters. They were very nice, and we called each other cousins and became very close. Of course, I called him Uncle. He was always very nice to me, always picking me up and giving me hugs. I was shocked that any friend of my public enemy number one liked me. Going over to their house was my way of escaping the misery I lived in at home.

However, their home was not a happy place for me either for long. On several occasions, while sleeping in the bed with my cousin, I would always make sure that I slept close to the wall. I was awakened several times when Uncle's hand reached over my cousin, and he would put his hand down my underwear, touching my vagina. He would wear a black robe and have a flashlight in his hand because the room was very dark.

I would always freeze up with paralyzing fear, not wanting him to know that I was awake. But, since I wanted his hands off me, I would move around as if

I was starting to wake up, and he would quickly remove his hand from my underwear. Then, I would lay on my stomach, stretching to purposely touch my cousin in hopes that she would awaken. But she never did, and he would leave once I turned over.

In the morning, I would feel sick to my stomach just looking at him, in that same robe, looking at me. I felt very violated but was too afraid to tell anyone because I didn't think that anyone would believe me. I was still confused as to why this kept happening to me. I must be doing something to ask for this because again, here was another adult I trusted because they always showed me what I thought was love. You would have thought I enjoyed the sexual abuse because I would continue to go over to his house. I remember having so much fear when I lived at home that Lucifer would carry through on his threats to kill me one day. I think that I would have been willing to stay overnight in the pit of hell before staying home. I always had a very hard time falling asleep at night, always going to bed scared that he was going to hurt my mom or me. I would have to rock myself back and forth while lying in bed in order to calm myself down before I could go to sleep.

My mother, somehow after getting two black eyes from one of his many beatings, found the courage to leave him. I was so proud of her. It was the happiest day of my life. It was on a school day; as my brother and I were getting ready for school, she was getting dressed as well. To my surprise, she was sober. She told Lucifer that she had an appointment somewhere. It was just my little brother and myself during our grammar school years, as our two older brothers were already at school. We were already standing at the bus stop when we saw our mom approaching us, wearing dark sunglasses. It was late fall, and there was no sun in sight. She was telling us to hurry and follow her. We were not going to school.

She held our hands while walking fast, causing my brother and me to run because we could not keep up. I was tired from running and was happy when we finally arrived at a center that helped battered women. Upon arrival, we were quickly placed in a room across from a lady sitting at a desk. My mother would not take her sunglasses off while talking to the lady. Someone brought in toys for my brother and me to play with. As my brother played, I kept my eyes on my mother. I was very worried about her. Although she was brave to go there, I could sense that she was scared.

While in the middle of the conversation with the counselor about all of the abuse, my mother fell out of her chair. She was having a seizure. The counselor stood there, screaming for help as my mom lay on the floor bucking, as she would call it. I had to tell the office staff what to do. She always told us if we saw her on the floor bucking to hurry and use a spoon to hold her tongue down so she didn't swallow it, until the bucking stopped. Then, she would always take a quick five or ten minute nap. As soon as it was over, she would open her eyes and talk to you. She would be back to herself again.

Although I had helped her through many seizures, I would still sometimes panic, especially if I was alone with her and she had been drinking. She was a crier when she was drunk, and stress always led her into one. I was afraid she would die on me because a friend's mother, who was one of my mother's drinking buddies, had died during a seizure. Although she was not able to be the mother that I needed all the time, I still loved her so much and wanted her around.

After my mom was better, my two older brothers were brought to the center, too. They put all of us in a white van with tinted windows and took us to a house far across town. We entered the house through the garage. It was filled with a diverse group of women and their children. The atmosphere was calm and felt safe.

We shared a room with another family. The room had two twin-sized beds for the mothers and bunk beds for the kids. Everyone ate in a huge kitchen with picnic tables, and we each had to take turns with cooking and cleaning. I felt like I was in a hotel! I had never stayed in a real hotel before, so this was luxury compared to the projects. We were all like one big, happy family. There was no arguing, cursing, or fighting, and my mom was sober every day. I thought I was in heaven. I made friends and saw my mom making new friends, but that was never a problem for her. She was known for being nice, outgoing, and giving. When someone she knew was sick, she would immediately take on the caregiver role.

My first professional haircut was done at this house. A salon came in to donate their services to the women and children. Not only did they want to take our minds off the fact that we were now homeless, but we were not allowed to go many places in public or tell anyone where we were staying. I begged and begged my mother to let me get my long, thick black hair that was down my back cut. She said no, and just wanted me to get it washed. But I wouldn't give up, so she gave in.

I was excited, so I ran to the salon area, sat down, and started looking through book after book for the right look. I waited for my turn to sit in the shampoo chair. I had a hard time picking a hairstyle because none of the pictures in the book had hair texture like mine, but everyone else's hairstyle looked nice, so I was not worried. When it was my turn in the chair, I showed the stylist the long, layered, feathered style on a beautiful red headed model that I wanted. She told me okay.

When given the mirror to see my finished look, I was mortified to see a four-inch afro. I left crying and went to my mother.

My mom had no sympathy at all. "Don't come crying to me, 'cause I told you so."

If that stylist came to try to cheer up some battered and abused women and kids, she had failed terribly.

The next day, I had to start a new school in the middle of the year. I was so nervous, and when I looked in the mirror, I felt as ugly as Mr. Boyfriend would always call me. I still loved staying at this home because I was able to sleep with both of my eyes closed. I actually saw my mother smile and laugh. It was like we had vanished from Buffalo. Lucifer had no idea where we were, and we were told not to contact anyone.

After being there for a month, we were told that the counselors were finding us a house and that we would be moving soon. I was excited at the thought of a fresh start, not ever having to see Mr. Boyfriend again, or come home to a mother with two black eyes, whom I could not help or even ask anyone to help without her cursing them and me out.

My world soon came crumbling down when my mother told us that she had talked with Lucifer and that we were going back to him. "How did he find out where we were?"

"I called him."

Now don't get me wrong; I loved my mother very much, never disrespected her, not even when she was drunk. I would have given my life for her. But at that moment, I told myself that she was the dumbest woman on the face of the earth to not only want to put herself back into an abusive relationship, but she was being selfish by making me go back to that hell hole where she knew I was hated. I was very disappointed in her.

Of course, things changed for about two weeks when we returned, but the beatings soon returned. I said that I would never be like her or my father when I grew up. I didn't understand, like I do now, the strong hold he had on her. It was not that she was dumb that kept her going back; it was that her self-esteem and self-worth were gone. In that weak state of mind, she felt like the beatings were normal and meant that he loved her and just didn't want to ever lose her, which made her feel special.

Meeting my Father

Shortly after we returned home from the battered women's house, my mother and I were walking down the street. Mom said to me, "There goes your daddy, across the street." My mother didn't want to call him over.

I was excited but did not know what to call him, so I called him by his first name. This tall man, with really skinny legs, turned around and took a look at us. While standing there, his weight shifted to his back leg, and to the other leg in front of him, with his arms folded across his chest. He had red-toned skin with a lot of thick hair hanging from under his cap. He was a very handsome man.

After he made the connection as to who I must be, he ran over to me. "Is this my Cordie Bee?" He gave me the biggest hug while picking me up. He was surprised at how much I had grown since I was now ten years old, and the last time he had seen me I was a baby. My mother left him and moved out of state because he used to beat her when he was drunk or high on drugs.

It felt so good to be held by my father. I could feel his love for me although he was absent for the majority of childhood. I still loved him and wanted to be part of his life. Even though I knew what he did to my mother, for some reason it was easier to forgive him than it was the boyfriend. There was something powerful about those biological genes, or maybe I was being like my mother, needing to feel loved by a male so much that I overlooked his wrong behavior.

My mother and father became friends again, and I was allowed to have a relationship with him. That's when I was able to meet my grandmother. My relationship with my father had its ups and downs but was cut short partly because we were a lot alike and because of his drug use. I used to get so angry with him out of fear for his life. I would watch him go in and out of this one apartment in our project that everyone knew was the crack house. I saw people being brought out of there dead.

The drug addiction prevented us from being close. If I did not give him money, when I was a working teenager, to support his habit, he would get very mad and swear at me. By then, words like that no longer bothered me because I knew where it was coming from. But I knew we loved each other, in our own way. I do have some memories of us getting along, laughing, and him taking me to Virginia to meet my other siblings. He used to give me rides on his motorcycle. I would walk to see him at the garage where he worked. He was a very good mechanic. If a car came in a box, he would have no problem putting it together.

My sister and I nicknamed him, "The Dollar Man," because anytime we asked for money, be it birthday, Christmas, or just because, all you got was one dollar. When you tried to squeeze more out of him, you would get this look and he would say,

"Mannn...." and walk away from you. I know for a fact that my dollars from him never totaled $50 our whole relationship, and we lived under the same roof when I lived with my grandmother, so I saw him every day.

I was not afraid of him; he never whipped me, just cussed me out because I would be mouthy to him sometimes. But he was nice, when he was high. But I still couldn't squeeze more than a dollar from him. One time, I was riding around in the car with him, his girlfriend (whom I loved), and my sister, when my father pulled over. He went and picked up this picture that someone had thrown out for trash.

I said, "What are you doing? Do not put that picture in this car! You don't know where it's been. And I don't want somebody else's trash touching me." Mind you, he had just picked me up from the projects, not the suburbs. I laugh now when I think about it because I do that now and love garage sales.

He was tired of my mouthing back, so my father reached back and grabbed one of my ponytails and yanked on it, which caused my mouth to shut as if I was a Muppet. I have to admit that I deserved that one.

Now as an adult, I understand that when people are addicted to drugs and alcohol it sometimes causes them to make decisions that they normally would not choose if the addiction was not there. My parents were good people who, unfortunately, chose this way to cope with life's problems. But, whatever the reasons were, their decisions had consequences that not only affected them, but also many others.

When Mom Joined Lucifer's Team

One time, I needed her to support me when I was wrongly accused by a neighbor who was one of her drinking buddies; she didn't believe me. The friend came and told Lucifer and my mom that she saw some other girls and me on the train tracks having sex with some boys. I was only about eleven and a half. Yes, I was with a group of girls and boys, and some of the kids did go off into the fields by the tracks. But Cordie had sex with no one. I was known as a tease to the boys because, although I liked boys and had boyfriends, I would only stay with them until they wanted sex; then, I would break up with them. My sexual abuse turned me off to the act because of fear, but I still liked having a boyfriend or two.

I tried to explain to my mom that it was not me having sex, but her boyfriend jumped in and said I was lying. He said that I was a fast acting little girl, but that's the clean version of the words he used. My mom, of course, chose to listen to my Public Enemy Number One. She took me to my room and whipped me with a belt. She made me lie down on the bed on my back and open my legs, and she hit me between my legs on my vagina. Now that was a whooping, out of many, that I would never forget. After she left my room, I could hear her telling him where she whipped me, and they were both laughing out loud. My nickname from my mother became "Hot Cox Sally." Every time she would call me that, I would feel, and still feel to this day, like a dirty, degraded hoe. After all, it was my fault for making nice men want to do bad things to me.

After that, I knew that my mom, whom I loved very much, was now on my enemy's team. My brothers were also now alone without any protection. He had complete control of her. The betrayal from my mom hurt so bad that I felt like I had a heart hemorrhage. Lucifer had taken not only my self-esteem, self-worth, dignity, confidence, childhood, family, and friends, but also my mother. Before him, my mom would cuddle with me in her bed, do my hair in pretty ponytails, and take me to the Goodwill to buy baby clothes for my dolls.

I would never stay home alone with him. One time, before I moved out because of him, I came home to find him drunk on the couch in his underwear. It was a summer night, around 9:30. No one else was home, and I had my friend with me. I was too scared to walk any closer to him, so I stood by the door and told him, "Mom said that my friend could stay overnight with me."

"I said no she can't." He told her to go home, and then said, "Get your *&%$#@* in here."

My heart began to pound as fight or flight began to take over me. "I'm going back down the street to mom and come home with her."

He started cursing and threatening me if I didn't come in the house. By this time, my friend was shaken, and she left quickly. I knew going into the

28

house alone, with him drunk, could not have been good for me. He had already hit me in the past, and I saw how he treated the woman he said that he loved. I didn't even need to imagine what he would do to me, being number one on his hit list.

He tried to get his drunken self off the couch to come and get me. I ran out of the house, jumping down four flights of stairs. My feet only touched the top and bottom of each landing with these red clogs on that only had one strap across my toes. I could hear him in the hallway of the apartment building, yelling out of the window at me. He told these boys that were hanging out in the court to grab me.

It took him some time to catch up with me, even in my clogs. I guess I was in full flight mode by then. When the boy caught up with me, I was a good distance from the house. "If you don't let go, I will tell my brothers on you." He let go.

Thinking that Lucifer was still coming after me, I continued to run and run as fast I could, not looking back once. I was running down the dangerous Genesee Street, which was known for a lot of shootings, wild bars, and prostitution. It was going on 10:30pm by then, and I did not have a clue as to where I was going. I just went wherever my feet took me. I was so scared that he was going to catch me. After about thirty minutes of sprinting in clogs, I started feeling like I was going to pass out. I found myself outside of a bar and spotted a police car sitting across the street patrolling the bar.

I went up to the officer and told him that my mother's boyfriend was after me and he was going to beat me up. I gave him his full name and asked him if he could please help me. I was shaking so bad and was frantic, thinking he was still running behind me.

It is amazing how I can remember that night so plainly, as if it happened yesterday. Picturing the bar, drunk people outside, and even how the police car was parked, but I can't remember the people I spent four years of high school with.

The officer had me get into the car and sat in the front seat. For the first time, I began telling him what happened. The history with my mom and her boyfriend, including him hitting my mother and me.

The officer actually said, "So you are afraid of a little spanking?"

"No, he will beat me bad."

"Is there a relative's house I can take you to?"

I told him, "Over to my aunt's house." As we arrived, my body went limp with fear. Even with this officer, I didn't feel safe. He carried me to her door, and my adult cousin answered the door. The officer told her that I was having problems at home and too scared to go back. He asked if I could stay there until the next day. He took me inside and laid me on the couch and he left. Then, I told her what had happened. She assured me that it was going to be all right and gave me a blanket and let me sleep on the couch.

I eventually fell asleep but was woken up around 4am by someone trying to climb in the window. The couch was in front of the window, but because it was dark, I couldn't see the person. I just knew I was dead because Lucifer must have found me. I jumped up screaming as I ran to my cousin's room, waking her up yet again. "Someone's trying to break into your house!"

She didn't appear alarmed as she got up and went into the living room and saw that it was just her boyfriend. Why, at twenty-something years old, this man did not just knock on the door, I had no idea. I just knew for a moment I had no heartbeat. Talk about creepy.

Being only twelve years old at the time, the officer told my mom where I was and that she could pick me up the next day to take me back home. No further questions asked; the legal system definitely failed me yet again. I was made to return to a house that my mom often referred to as the "Hell Hole."

She was right about that; it was truly where Satan sat on his throne.

There were times when my mother wanted out of that relationship but just didn't have the courage to leave him. Oftentimes, I saw her so broken, crying uncontrollably, that she told me that voices in her head would tell her to go to the roof of our apartment building and jump off so she could go home to be with her mother. She had died when my mom was only eleven years old.

Mom had told me that back then, funerals were held in your house, with the casket in the living room. Her mother's casket was brought into the house, but the funeral was not until the next day. That night, my mom cried herself to sleep on top of her mother's casket and stayed there until the next day. My heart breaks for her as I think of how alone she must have felt.

I had heard many suicidal threats, but I can only remember one that she actually attempted. One day, while her boyfriend was out somewhere, probably getting drunk, my brothers and I were home alone with her. We sat watching cartoons, and she came out of the bathroom, walking very calmly, sat on the couch, and said, "I just took a whole bunch of pills."

My brothers and I didn't know what to make of it, since we were young. We just looked at her as if to say, "Okay", and looked back at the cartoons.

Mom yelled, "Fools!" It was one of her favorite words to call you. "Y'all better call the ambulance before I die, cause I ain't playing!"

We all jumped up in a panic, dialing 911. She was taken to the hospital and had her stomach pumped. From that day forward, I was afraid to leave her alone, but also afraid to be alone with her. I was scared that I wouldn't know how to help her. I lived in constant fear.

Conforming to My Environment

By the time I was in the 7th grade, I was getting drunk and smoking reefer. After all, it was all around me. We had more vodka in the house than milk or toothpaste. My friends and I would put our change together and walk to the corner store. We would wait outside until we saw a wino. We would offer to buy him a bottle of Wild Irish Rose, which was one of the cheapest wines you could buy back then, if he got us a bottle. Or, we would offer to buy him a forty-ounce bottle of beer if he bought each of us one. One time, I actually drank just about a whole bottle myself, with my friends in my bedroom.

Mom and her boyfriend were in the living room, drunk and asleep. Mom was on the couch, and Lucifer was on the carpet-less floor. I had to step over him to get to my room. That day, I was so drunk I could not walk. I woke up the next day, feeling sick to death. My head felt like someone was trying to crack a watermelon open with a hammer, stomach cramping severely, and I couldn't stop vomiting.

I have always been the type of person that refused to go to the hospital or doctor. I would just tough it out when I felt sick. But this time, I asked my mom to take me.

"If you're asking to go, you must be really sick."

We didn't have a car, so anytime we needed to go to the ER, it was always by ambulance. I hated the attention, because everybody would come out of their apartments and just stand there watching you.

Once in the ER, the doctor kept asking me over and over if I drank alcohol. I continued to lie, telling them no, even after the doctor put a nasogastric tube down my nose and into my stomach. He pointed out that the continuous yellow liquid flowing through the tube was poison from alcohol. Never telling the truth, my mother left me after she was told that I had to stay overnight. She believed me.

I was alone in my hospital room, crying, because I was sure I was going to die. The hospital chaplain came into my room. I was convinced that he was specifically sent to talk to the people who were dying, including me. He started asking me if I drank alcohol. I continued to lie. I began to cry harder as he prayed for me. At that time, I didn't know a lot about God, just that he was someone who lives in the sky that you called on when you needed help. After the chaplain left, I did pray and promised God that if he let me live, I would never drink again.

> **BUT AS FOR YOU, YE THOUGHT EVIL AGAINST ME; BUT GOD MEANT IT UNTO GOOD, TO BRING TO PASS, AS IT IS THIS DAY, TO SAVE MUCH PEOPLE ALIVE.**
> **(Genesis 50:20, King James Version)**

That is one promise I kept.

As a young teenager, I continued to try to stay out of my mom's house as much as possible by staying with different friends, even out of town relatives. I would often live back and forth from my brother's house, after he had moved out, to my mother's house for maybe a month at a time. Usually not too much longer than that, because they were both young parents who were struggling to take care of their little families.

My mother was in such a dark place mentally that she had no fear of death. I heard her give her boyfriend the okay to kill her one day when he threatened to do it. They were both sitting on the couch; my little brother and I were standing in front of them, with the coffee table between us. It was filled with shot glasses that they stole from the bars and ash trays filled with cigarette butts. They were both drunk, and Lucifer had a gun in his hands and told us that he was going to shoot our mother.

Then he told us to go stand in the hallway in a calm voice. There was no yelling or screaming going on; I'm not sure what led up to it. My brother and I began crying and were told to give her a hug as we walked to the front door that led out to the hallway. I watched my mom sit there, with no tears, no fear. She was completely emotionless as she sat next to him. We got halfway out the door; Lucifer called us back in, looking at our terrified faces. "Awww, you don't want me to kill your mother."

What a sick man.

I was even sold for a pack of cigarettes. There was this guy who was about twenty-five years old who lived across the court from my building. He would always stare at me. One day, while walking past, he

35

was hanging out of his window and he called me over. He asked me to come upstairs to his apartment to watch a movie with him. Even though I told him no, he continued on pressing me. He kept saying that he just wanted to be friends and I didn't have anything to worry about. Not only was I not interested in him, I also knew he was too old since I was only about thirteen years old.

While standing there trying to figure out how to get away from talking with him, my mom stuck her head out our window. I was relieved; this was my chance to get away from him. "I have to ask my mother." Most of the time I didn't, because she didn't know where I was. She was unable to stay sober, so I was free to go wherever I wanted, no questions asked.

I know God was with me back then because I was in many places that a teenager shouldn't have been allowed to go. Thank you, Lord, for your covering. Anyway, I was sure that with him being so much older, he would back down and not ask her, but he did.

To my surprise, she said, "Yes, if you buy me a pack of cigarettes."

Talk about feeling cheap and less than. So they sent me to the store, like the good little girl that I was, and I brought the cigarettes back to my mother. I gave her a look as if to say, "I can't believe that you are okay with this." She didn't know anything about him, except where he lived.

I didn't feel like he was going to rape me, but I just knew that it was inappropriate. My mother should have said no, using some of those many cuss words she often used on me. It was really creepy. Thank God he did not force himself on me, but I just could not sit there any longer with him constantly telling me how beautiful I was. Him staring at me with those beady eyes made my skin crawl. I was very street smart, and I knew all the compliments. He wanted to make a movie with me, not watch one. I agreed to kiss him, then I had to leave. Those were the worst French kisses I ever had. He was a smoker, so it tasted like what I think an old, rusted pipe would taste like.

Meant for Evil

One day when I was fifteen years old, I got home from school, and my mom told me to stop right there. No hello, no how was school, she just told me how her boyfriend and I didn't get along and one of us would have to go, and "My man ain't going nowhere." I stood there with my backpack still on, looking at her shocked and confused. It's not like I told her man off the night before. I was too scared to do that. With my heart torn to pieces that she chose him over me, I didn't know what I was going to do. I was definitely the worst person in the world because not even my mother wanted me.

At that moment, I felt as if life was no longer important; why did God allow me to be born? I reminded her that I was her child and it should be him that leaves. Her response was very sarcastic when she said, "You can't take care of me."

I was so devastated that we were even having this conversation. This was the one time I wished that she had been drunk or high. I think that I would have been able to process it better, but she was very much sober and serious. "Mom, it should be the other way around," I said, even though I felt like I was often the parent in our relationship, trying so hard to protect her. Always worrying about her safety. "You are supposed to take care of me. Plus, he doesn't take care of you either. He has no job. You give him the money you get from welfare for having four kids, remember?" She still insisted that I leave, so I did, not grabbing any clothes, never to return.

After I left, I crossed the street in a daze as to what had just happened. Not paying attention to the cars as I crossed, I remember a car with its horn blowing at me. I was thinking I didn't even care if the car hit me. The driver might actually be doing me a favor. I didn't speed up my pace and just kept walking. I didn't know God at that time, but he knew me and had a purpose for me. That's why he protected me and got me to the other side of the street safely.

The only place I knew to go was to my father's mother's house, so I caught a bus to Grandmother's house. I arrived there in tears. To my surprise, my mother knew that was exactly where I would go. She had called before I got there and told my grandmother to not allow me to live there. My grandmother was very upset with my mom for putting me out over a man, not really giving her a reason besides saying that I couldn't come back home.

My grandmother called Child Protective Services. After the social worker arrived, we sat in the living room while the social worker asked a lot of questions. When the social worker asked my grandmother if she wanted to keep me or to allow me to go with the social worker, my grandmother looked at me, puzzled, and said, "I can't answer these questions in front of her."

The caseworker asked me to leave the room, but before I left, I said, "It's okay, I can go with her. I don't even care."

My grandmother decided to allow me to stay with her, but I know she had some apprehension because she was not able to get around like she used to, as she was in a wheelchair. She was also concerned about raising a teenager, knowing she would have no help from her son. I was fifteen years old when I went to live with Grandma. I never returned to my mom's house again.

While living with my grandmother, I got to meet one of my uncle's ex-girlfriends. She remained good friends with my grandmother. This family friend would come over every Sunday after church, looking so pretty in her church clothes and driving her nice car. There was such an elegance and peaceful spirit about her that caught my attention. I also noticed that she didn't smoke, drink, or cuss like many of my grandmother's other visitors.

One day, this friend of my grandmother's, who was a missionary, invited me to an event that the young people were having at her church. I went and was in awe at the abundance of young people my age, and even younger. I saw people in the church praising and worshiping God. I wanted what they had because they looked happy on the inside, something I never had.

After the service, I knew I wanted to come back, so I did. Again and again, until eventually this missionary picked me up for church every Sunday, Tuesday, and Friday. One Friday night, I had decided that this would be the day that I would accept Christ into my heart and surrender my life over to him. I wanted to go to heaven, and I had to have this joy that they talked about God giving you when you let him into your heart because the only thing in my heart was hurt, pain, anger, and a whole lot of sadness.

I walked up to the alter when the invitation to accept Christ was given. I was so scared that everyone was watching me and that I wouldn't do the right thing to get him in my heart. It just looked like it was something very hard to get. I was standing there with my eyes closed, tuning out my surroundings. Someone began whispering in my ear what to say, and I began to feel like I was standing before him, and it was just him and me in the room. I was just telling him that I didn't understand what I had done so wrong to make people hurt me. To make my parents not want to be around me. I wanted to be forgiven and change. I wanted to be a different person. I wanted to be a nice person. I wanted to be happy. I wanted that joy. I wanted to feel loved. I wanted to be able to feel. I wanted to care. I wanted him to live in my heart. I wanted to be able to feel his presence and feel his arms around me. I wanted to be saved and filled with the Holy Spirit.

After fighting through the tears, while asking for forgiveness and just talking to him like he was the daddy I never had, as the tears poured out of my eyes, my stomach began to do flips. I felt such an overwhelming chill go through my body. It was as if his arms were wrapped around me and his presence had just sent the Holy Spirit through my whole body. I knew he was touching me because I'd never felt like this before. For the first time, I can truly say I felt love, and I didn't want it to end. I continued to cry out to him, begging him to fill me. I just kept repeating, "fill me, Jesus, fill me, Jesus." The more I said that, the more I felt like I needed to spit up. I felt embarrassed and was thinking, "Oh, my gosh, I'm about to spit up on the church carpet and everyone will see!"

With spit coming out of my mouth, the person that was in my ear kept coaching me through and helping to keep me focused and connected with God. They told me not to worry about the spit and to let it out. They said God was just cleaning my temple so that he could come in. I could feel my mouth being cleaned, like a loving mother would for her child. God's word promises that he will cleanse us, like in Psalm 51:7, where it says,

> ## PURGE ME WITH HYSSOP, AND I SHALL BE CLEAN: WASH ME, AND I SHALL BE WHITER THAN SNOW.
> ## (Psalms 51:7, King James Version)

I could feel the love from the people as the spit was being wiped from my mouth, which encouraged me to continue to press for complete deliverance from God. I could hear them worshiping and rejoicing as they watched God touching me and transforming an unbeliever.

After acknowledging God had forgiven and saved me, he was now living in my heart along with the Holy Spirit. I continued to come to church in search of more and more of him. Although I continued to fall many times back into sin during this walk, I always got back up to continue to fight, because he is worth it. Thank God for his great mercy with me, as I asked for forgiveness many times. As I grew in Christ, I became more aware of my parents' eternal destiny in hell if they didn't change their lifestyles. I would cry every night as I prayed for them. I began to develop a fear of getting a call in the middle of the night. Of being told that they had died before they received Christ. It was so stressful on me that every time I was in their presence, I would just get depressed knowing their destiny and being unable to get them to accept Christ.

I finally got to the point where I realized God loved them more than I could, and I had to pray for them and release them to God. It was robbing me of my promised joy. I don't remember the exact day it happened, but I do remember God lifting that burden from me. I never stopped praying for them, always desiring and hoping that they would be born again, in hopes that we would have a better relationship.

God began to make me a human magnet, drawing those people who have been through similar situations. It gave me the opportunity to tell my story to those people who would always be surprised thinking that I could have never had such a childhood. That is when God showed me that this life is not my own. We go through things for other people. God allowed that because he knew that I would make it out. Then, this would be my calling, that I would have a heart and a passion for hurting people. I try my hardest to encourage others to hang in there through their struggles, to put their trust in God, and ask him to show them the whys for their struggles. I am still saved to this day, continually growing as a wife and with my husband, leading our children to God. I am completely devoted to availing myself to be used by God to win others over to him.

But just when I thought my living foundation would be firm, my grandmother became sick and was hospitalized. Aware of her failing health, Grandma made arrangements for me to live with the missionary who had been taking me to church so I could be supervised. By age seventeen, I was living with a family friend who became my godmother. By this time, I was an adult mentally because I had been in that role since I was a child. I was used to a home of dysfunction, chaos and no structure. It was very hard for me to adapt to a structured environment with a lot of rules, although that's what I wanted.

My teenage hormones also played a part in my decision to move out. I definitely had a problem with staying still. Feeling like an adult, now that I was out of high school, I was still living from house to house. I was tired of dragging garbage bags around, throwing them behind people's couches as I slept on them. I wanted stability! I decided that the only way I would have that would be to get my own house, but I was afraid of living alone, especially in the neighborhoods where I knew my public assistance money would be enough.

Not knowing which direction to go in making this happen, I went to the leaders of my church for advice. Thank God for giving them the wisdom to see that I was not ready for my own house yet and leading them to open up their home to me, and imparting some well-needed wisdom. However, after the passing of my pastor, I begin to feel like I was a burden living there. I was never told that from the first lady, and I still felt loved. But it was God's way of pushing me out because it was finally time to learn to walk on my own. Now, in my early twenties, I was finally on my own, living in my own house, no one telling me what to do. I loved my small apartment. I finally had peace! There's nothing like your own home. I lived in my own apartment for about two years before marrying.

My father's neglect, due to his drug and alcohol addictions, taught me to not be like him. I learned a lot of the games men like to play on women. He often made me feel like I was his least favorite child because of our struggles in our relationship. But it also taught me that you should never show favorites among your children. When you are in true need of your children, it's often the one you least expect that is loyal. When my parents died, I felt like I was left to carry all the guilt of our broken relationships.

God Meant for Good

Just when I thought love wasn't possible, I met my future husband. We saw each other at the vocational high school we both attended. I was in the nursing program and he was in the cosmetology program. It was amazing how God had it to be; I was learning how to take care of the inside of people; he was learning how to take care of the outside.

We never spoke more than hi or bye, until I came to the salon where he worked. When I booked the appointment, I didn't realize it was going to be with this same guy from school. I was referred by a friend from church. When I got in his chair, we had a great conversation about church travels and our relationship with the Lord. In spite of all the people that were around, it felt like we were the only two in the room.

The appointment took a long time; however, it felt too short. At the time of my appointment, we both were in a relationship with other people. Soon after my first appointment, however, Steven broke off his long distance relationship that he'd been in. Between March 1991 and January 1992, I had a few more appointments, but when I came to the salon I found my feelings were very mixed. Sometimes, I felt like he liked me; other times I felt like I wasn't so sure. I was wondering if he was just an overall nice guy.

I later found out he was reluctant to approach me because he did not want me to feel like he came on to all of his clients. I started gaining feelings for him during that time, but I was still in a relationship with someone else. That relationship was very strained and it felt more like a mercy relationship. I tried to break it off several times, but my boyfriend's mother kept advocating for us to stay together.

Fast forward to January of the following year; I received a surprising phone call. I was on the phone with my boyfriend. When I switched over, Steven was on the line. He invited me to a skating party his job was sponsoring. We started having a really good conversation, then it went deep. He started to pour out his feelings towards me. He told me he was absolutely crazy about me. After he poured out his heart to me, I was shocked.

I asked him, "What took so long?"

He told me that he was reluctant to come on to me out of fear of scaring me away. That conversation lasted for a couple hours. My boyfriend was on the other line and I never switched back over to continue our conversation.

I had dreams, even though I grew up in an environment with no successful examples. Not even my friends' parents went to college. I rarely saw nurses who looked like me when I went to the hospitals. It has always concerned me that I knew at a young age that I wanted to be a nurse. I felt it deep in my soul, even though my environment said that people like me, and where I was from, don't become nurses. I didn't know how, or even if I could, but knew that I had to try. But I was so intimidated by the thought of a nursing career.

I often wondered why I could not have a burning in my soul to become something less complicated. I had such a love for sick people, but was being told constantly that I was dumb and ugly, or called a nobody. Not to mention when my mother told me that I didn't even have a mother during those times when I would go to the house unannounced, when she and her friends were doing drugs. She wouldn't even open the door. I asked her to stop doing the drugs and let me in. She would just tell me to go away, that she didn't want to hear about God. Even though I knew where it was coming from, it would still cut and hurt, leaving scars.

My dream of becoming a registered nurse seemed as impossible as a trip from earth to Mars on foot. I was always using my dolls as patients that I would have to nurse back to health. I was still doing this all the way up to 8th grade, when most of my friends were done playing with dolls. Some of them even had real babies. My grandmother took care of elderly people in her home. I would feel sorry for them because they had no family of their own that came to visit them. Our family treated them as family, bringing whatever they asked for. Sometimes, I would take a tray to their room and sit and talk with them. I'd take a red bingo marker, and they'd let me put a mark on their arm and pretend it was blood and then bandage it up. They enjoyed my company, and I enjoyed the pretend play. I always had a heart for the weak, needy, sick, the elderly and babies.

My main motivation to complete college was being determined to not be like my parents. Before my grandmother died, I had made her a promise that

I would become a nurse. She was the only one I felt who believed in me. I graduated from high school and a vocational tech program without the support of either of my biological parents. Neither were there, even though they were living and knew about my graduation. It broke my heart. I do thank God for blessing me with mother-like figures, cousins, brothers, and a sister who did come to support me. But there is still something about the biological genes that keeps you hoping, even when there is every reason not to. To God be all the glory for me finally making it out of high school.

With college on my mind, I knew deep in my soul that God had something better for me.

FOR I KNOW THE THOUGHTS THAT I THINK TOWARD YOU, SAITH THE LORD, THOUGHTS OF PEACE, AND NOT OF EVIL, TO GIVE YOU AN EXPECTED END. (Jeremiah 29:11, King James Version)

I felt I could become a nurse deep in my soul, as if it was part of my DNA. But I did not believe it in my head, that I was smart enough. Nursing was one of the toughest majors you could take in college. I was very intimidated by a four-year college. I decided a community college was more my speed, until I enrolled and found out that what a university teaches in four years, I only had two to learn and prepare to take the same nursing board exam. That was a nightmare for me.

49

I did not grow up with books in the home. My parents never bought me books, nor read a book to me. The first book I read from beginning to end was my Psychology 101 book in college. After I was enrolled in the nursing program and saw my nursing book that was as thick as a telephone book, I was really sure that I would not make it through. But something inside me would not let me give up, even after failing and having to repeat one of my nursing classes.

Friends began to ask if I was going to school to be a doctor or if I was sure God wanted me to be a nurse because it was taking me so long to graduate from a community college. Thank God I made it through. Unfortunately, my grandmother and father were both deceased by then, and my mother still did not attend my graduation. I'm sure her staying away was part guilt and part her way of trying to protect me from her lifestyle. She was just not strong enough to win the fight against it. I do forgive her, though. I was the only child my parents had together, so I thought it would have made her happy knowing that out of her wrong decisions, I was still able to graduate college, giving her an opportunity to attend a college graduation for the first time.

Satan Tries to Take Me Out

I was on my way out of this world as my baby was on his way in. Satan was still trying to stop the will of God that was placed on my life by taking me out. I was very happy on the day my husband came from work and I was able to tell him that our efforts of trying to conceive a baby were successful. God had blessed us to be pregnant. Prior to our pregnancy, I was a very healthy person taking no medication. However, early in my first trimester I became very sick, overtaken with what is called "morning sickness," but in my case it was 24-hour sickness. I was no longer able to keep food or water down; eventually even ice chips came back up. After becoming severely dehydrated, I was hospitalized for a week and later discharged with nurses coming to my home to give me IV therapy.

My sickness continued to worsen as I moved into my second trimester, still unable to keep food down and losing body fluids daily through diarrhea, excessive spitting, and vomiting. Ladies, if you have experienced the spitting issue, I am sure you can relate to how gross and annoying this was. I remember being so weak I could barely hold my spit cup. One time, I dropped it and I had to get my husband to clean it up. I felt so bad and was not used to anyone taking care of me. When my husband saw my slimy mess, instantly gagging he stated, "You hate me, don't you?" But being the wonderful husband that he is, he cleaned it up.

My vomiting was even worse with nothing on my stomach but gastric juices and IV fluids. It turned into projectile vomiting, causing my job to send me home. I had made a mess in our employee bathroom more than once. They told me to not return until after I had the baby. I was still early in my second trimester. Of course this continued fluid loss led to more hospitalization and continued IV therapy, to the point where my husband became a pro at changing my IV bag at 3 o'clock in the morning when the IV pump alarm would go off.

By the middle of my second trimester, preeclampsia had set in. By the 27th week of my pregnancy, my blood pressure was rocket high. I literally felt like I was dying. I mean, I could feel death to the point of when, lying in the bed at night I would pray, "Lord, please do not allow my young husband to wake up to a deceased, pregnant wife." I did not want that to be part of his testimony.

One morning, I called the doctor, informing him how abnormally sick I felt. He tried to reassure me that I was only twenty-seven weeks along and that the feelings were normal for a first pregnancy. It was because I was dehydrated and had preeclampsia. He told me to lie down and put my feet up. That's when God told me that something was wrong, that this was not normal. I needed to get to the doctor.

I called the doctor back and insisted that I come into the office; he reluctantly gave me an appointment. He told me that I would have to wait a very long time because he was very busy that day. After arriving at the doctor's office and sitting in the waiting room for about one hour, my blood pressure was taken and it was 190/126. Well, needless to say, that shut the office down. I was taken to the emergency room with the doctor following after me. I was told to call my husband to meet me at the hospital because I needed to have an emergency c-section.

Remember, a full-term pregnancy is close to forty weeks, and I was only twenty-seven weeks. My preeclampsia had now reached what is called the HELLP Syndrome. HELLP Syndrome is a life-threatening pregnancy complication, usually considered to be a variant of preeclampsia. The H stands for hemolysis, which is the breaking down of red blood cells, EL stands for elevated liver enzymes, and LP is low platelet count. The mortality rate of HELLP syndrome has been reported to be as high as 25%. That's why it's critical for expecting mothers with high blood pressure and protein in their urine to be aware of the condition and its symptoms so they can receive early diagnosis and treatment.

The most common reasons for mothers to become critically ill, or die, are liver rupture or stroke (cerebral edema or cerebral hemorrhage). Basically, to sum it up, it's your body shutting down on you, and the only way to save your life and your baby is to end the pregnancy. My husband was being told that he could lose his wife and baby. We were very scared, and my husband began calling the Saints to pray. Now at the hospital, while being prepped for an emergency c-section, the excitement of being a new father begin to overshadow the seriousness of my condition. He began calling more friends and family, excitedly telling them that the baby was coming and I was okay.

After my nursing skills began to kick in, I did not want to ruin my husband's excitement about our son coming. I did not share with him that I knew the medical staff thought that I was going to die. Although the medical staff tried to keep the seriousness of my condition from me, I knew by them padding my side rails they feared me having a seizure or stroke. They hung additional medication bags on my IV pole to help bring my blood pressure down, and the fact that my nurse said that he was not allowed to leave my room all added to the seriousness. My husband counted at least ten injections into my back to get my epidural going. The doctors had a hard time getting the needles in due to the fifty pounds of water gain, thirty of which were lost during my seven-day hospitalization after our first son was born at two pounds and seven ounces.

To God be the glory for yet again sparing my life. When I came back to visit our son, who was unable to go home with us for a while, I saw one of the doctors in the elevator. He looked at me and said, "I can't believe I'm looking at you in the elevator. We were sure that we were going to lose you that night you delivered a baby."

Now that's called purpose in my life. God continued to fulfill His purpose in my life by blessing me through my second pregnancy with preeclampsia, and my third pregnancy being hospitalized with a blood clot. I had to take injections in my abdomen while I was pregnant. My church family began to think that I had a death wish with my additional pregnancies. After my near-death experience with my first son, my mother had told me not to have any more kids, fearing that I might die giving birth like her sister did.

What she didn't understand was that my husband I were in prayer for each one of our pregnancies. They were planned, and God had told me that my family was not complete until our third child was here. After my third child and I almost died after having the blood clot, which was high in my pelvis, once again, another doctor came to me and told me that someone up there in the sky loves me. I knew exactly who he was talking about, God! Instead of asking God, "Why do bad things often happen to me?" these experiences made me more determined to grow more in him as he fulfills his will that he has for my life. I am determined to pray and tell as many people as I can about his goodness, about his mercy, his grace, his love, and that life is meaningless without him.

Growing Pains

As a young Christian, I did believe God when he said,

> ## I CAN DO ALL THINGS THROUGH CHRIST WHICH STRENGTHENETH ME.
> ## (Philippians 4:13, King James Version)

but fear of failure did paralyze me from going to retake my boards for the third time. I had allowed years of being told that I was a nobody and stupid to take over my life. After five years had passed, I could no longer take the dull, aching void, and the jealous feeling I had when I talked to my many nursing friends, or someone in a nurse's uniform. I began to give my fear to God, telling myself,

> ## THE LORD IS MY LIGHT AND MY SALVATION, WHOM SHALL I FEAR?
> ## (Psalm 27:1a, King James Version)

Retaking the state boards will not be the end of the world if I fail it again. It is only a test.

I began to thank God for what he had already done for me in those five years. He had given me a loving husband and spared my life with two near death experiences during childbirth. The doctors were telling me that they thought I was going to die, and honestly when you are that close to it, you can feel death is near. It is hard to explain to those who are around you, but at the time, you know it. I found the courage to dust those nursing books off and retake my RN state board. The school said, because of the many years between graduation and retaking it, I only had a 1% chance of passing. Whose report do you think I believed? To God I give all the glory for blessing me and passing my Registered Nursing Boards. We serve a powerful God.

When I stopped focusing on where I came from and who I was told I could not be and put my focus on the new creation God had made me to be, I realized it was all just a part of my journey to get there. That was when I was able to pass my RN state boards. However, low self-esteem still had its dirty paws on me. Even with my nursing license in hand and my supervisors always applauding my work performance, I still felt inferior to the other nurses, never fitting in with them, but the love for the sick and dying people kept me returning to that very stressful environment.

I now know that through all that hell (sorry, but there is no nicer word I could use to describe my youth), God was still there all the time. He only allowed Satan to test me, but did not give him the permission to kill me, although there were times I wanted Satan to take me out and death would have been a treat for me.

I often asked the Lord, "Why me?" He answered with, "Because I have predestined you from your mother's womb for this assignment. I have created you, so I know that you will come out as an overcomer." I never thought that a strong woman could come from a very weak, broken, and unstable foundation. That is because God is so awesome! He has also said to me:

AND HE SAID UNTO ME, MY GRACE IS SUFFICIENT FOR THEE: FOR MY STRENGTH IS MADE PERFECT IN WEAKNESS. MOST GLADLY THEREFORI WILL I RATHER GLORY IN MY INFIRMITIES, THAT THE POWER OF CHRIST MAY REST UPON ME. THEREFORE I TAKE PLEASURE IN INFIRMITIES, IN REPROACHES, IN NECESSITIES, IN PERSECUTIONS, IN DISTRESSES FOR CHRIST'S SAKE: FOR WHEN I AM WEAK, THEN AM I STRONG I AM BECOME A FOOL IN GLORIFYING; YE HAVE COMPELLED ME: FOR I OUGH' TO HAVE BEEN COMMENDED OF YOU: FOR IN NOTHING AM I BEHIND THE VERY CHIEFEST APOSTLES, THOUGH I BE NOTHING.
(2 Corinthians 12:9-11, King James Version)

There were many times I was like Paul, very self-sufficient. I was so focused on being strong and always said that I would never let a man know that I needed him. When my husband and I started dating, I was in college. Talk about being broke. I was broker than broke, living on my own. My bed was a fold up, roll-away bed, like the ones you sleep on when you go stay in the shelters. My dresser was made of multiple boxes stacked on top of each other, and I had to take them down each time I needed to get different items out.

When my husband was still just my boyfriend, he was very successful in his career, working crazy long hours and making very good money. He would often ask if I had money, and I would say yes, with only a dollar in my purse and getting behind on my cable bill. Instead of allowing him to pay my bills, I had the cable turned off and lived without it. Even if I had a quarter in my pocket, not telling him how much I had, I never asked him to do anything for me. I was just determined to not be dependent upon any man.

That was my defense, not trusting men and waiting on them to leave me for someone else. After all, I didn't feel worthy of being married because if my parents couldn't show me love, I must not be lovable. I was sure one day he would abandon me as well. Thanks be to God for showing my husband something in me that I didn't even see in myself. As of 2014, we have celebrated eighteen years of marriage. He always tells me if he had to pick again, he would marry me all over again. Now those words melt my heart.

I have to admit, when we first got married, I was very intimidated by his profession of working with nothing but pretty and successful women. I asked

God, "Now, why would you give me a man that has to be around nothing but women? His phone filled with women's names and numbers that I don't even know. Lord, you know I suffer with low self-esteem." That is exactly how our father works; he puts us in situations that break us in order to make us.

God said, "I gave him to show you how beautiful, special, and lovable you really are. Out of those many women who have sat in his chair, at the end of the day, he comes home to you." God also used my husband to work on me with my trust issues. You definitely have to have trust being married to a hair stylist and musician. Isn't our God awesome?

Our life is not our own; we belong to God.

> ## YE HAVE NOT CHOSEN ME, BUT I HAVE CHOSEN YOU, AND ORDAINED YOU, THAT YE SHOULD GO AND BRING FORTH FRUIT, AND THAT YOUR FRUIT SHOULD REMAIN: THAT WHATSOEVER YE SHALL ASK OF THE FATHER IN MY NAME, HE MAY GIVE IT TO YOU.
> ### (John 15:16, King James Version)

Effects of Addiction

I now understand that the neglect from my parents was due in part to their addiction. If you have loved ones struggling with addictions, they oftentimes stay away because they are embarrassed, ashamed, and because of their love for you. That's their way of protecting you from themselves.

When I was younger, I thought my mother and father chose to be addicted to drugs. I thought that their love for me should have been stronger than their addiction. It was as if I looked at the addiction as another child that they loved more than me, which led to my insecurity. If I only could have been a better person, they would have loved me more.

A person with addictions is unable to be faithful to love. Any addiction is a self-destructive disease that robs you from loving yourself, destroys your life and the life of others. My parents, at times, wanted to be free from their addictions, but due to their lack of strength and unwillingness to completely surrender their lives over to God, they failed. This is not something that you can beat on your own. It not only takes your strong will of wanting deliverance, but most importantly, it takes a life in Christ.

Although I wanted them to be delivered, at a very young age, I learned their manipulative ways and I refused to be an enabler. It often led to them being very upset with me because I didn't give in to their wants. Standing my ground, as hard as it was, I had to accept this was the lifestyle they chose. God gives us all the same choices, even though he can make us choose the right one. I came to accept their choice and their lifestyle; however, I had to set barriers so that I was no longer hurt and to protect my family. I learned to pray and to love them from a distance.

The Victory

My prayer as a teenager was, "Lord, please bless me with a family of my own that truly loves me and let my husband treat me like a princess." Proverbs 18:22a (King James Version) says,

> ## WHOSO FINDETH A WIFE FINDETH A GOOD THING.
> ## (Proverbs 18:22a, King James Version)

so I waited on God. He gave me just what I needed in a husband, someone with a big heart, compassion, soft-spoken, outgoing, and a go-getter. My husband is my best friend and knows how to put to rest every insecurity that tries to come up in me. His presence alone calms my anxieties. Our love is deeply rooted and soul tying, connected with God.

It has not always been that way. When we first met, that little girl in me rose up, unknowingly expecting him to be the father I never had and treat me like his little princess. What pressure I had put on him. I came with a lot of baggage. When I felt his true love for me, early in our courtship, I had a hard time believing him, thinking he must not know what love is. In my mind, it was going to take years, and even a visit from God in the flesh, to assure me that it was okay to open my heart up to this man. Dating for five years, it was very important that he know that I did not need him getting me anything. I had my own apartment that I lived in for two years before we got married. During that time, I was so self-sufficient; I was so focused on being strong and not needing anyone, not friends and especially not a man. I had always said that I would never let my husband know that I needed him. I now understand that was my defense mechanism against my abandonment and rejection issues. I was fearful he would leave me for someone else. After all, I did not feel worthy of being married because if my parents couldn't show me love, I must be unlovable.

The Depression

My mother died in a tragic drowning when the car she was in flipped over into a river, pinning my mother and her girlfriend in it, upside down. I was told that some highway workers heard them screaming from the car and had tried to get her and the driver out before the car was completely submerged under water. They were unsuccessful, and my mother and her girlfriend drowned.

When I saw my mother in the casket, I could tell that the windows of the car had to be broken in order to get them out, as she had little cuts on her face from the glass. My life did a 360 back to my childhood, and all of a sudden, I was that little girl who was waiting and praying for her mother to get her life together so I could have a chance, as a child, for a close relationship and to feel much love from my mother. I was devastated that my fantasy was now never going to happen. It still brings tears to my eyes as I type this.

I was in denial, thinking things like, "No! She can't be gone forever. I have so many questions I need to be answered. Now who is going to take care of this little girl that is still inside me that still needs her chance at childhood?" That little girl needed to be told that all the bad things that were said and done to her were not her fault. She needed to feel her mommy's arms around her and be told that she is beautiful, smart, loved, and important.

Married with children of my own, this little girl on the inside of me still desperately needed her. Because of all the days I had to take care of my mother when she was drunk, assisting her through her many seizures, taking care of myself while being worried about being hurt on a daily basis, that little girl had stopped growing at about seven years old. I had to become the parent in our relationship, and that had been my role ever since. Now that she was gone, I felt like I was the bad parent and my child was killed in an automobile accident and it was my fault. I did not protect her. What a heavy burden I carried for years, without people knowing. I was a master at suppressing my feelings to the extreme. I could store those painful thoughts so far in the back of my mind, it was as if I erased them completely. Yes, even as a Christian that was my coping mechanism.

The pain of her sudden death was too painful for me to deal with. It was more painful than I thought since I was filled with guilt for not having a close relationship. Although our lack of relationship was not all my fault, because I was not the one gone, I was left to carry the guilt load for the both of us.

I was in such a very low place, both mentally and emotionally, that although I was a Christian and living my life completely for Christ, I didn't have enough strength to pull from that place Christ has in my heart. Has your pain ever been so severe that you could not get a prayer out of your mouth? I am talking about feeling so numb that you feel nothing, not even feeling the Holy Spirit coming to your rescue? Due to the pain in my heart, I felt so low that I could not even utter a prayer. I knew how to pray, but I felt numb, like God had left me alone, or as if he had a deaf ear to my prayers.

Still not accepting my mother's death, I kept her home number in my phone, even calling it on occasion, as if she was still living out of town and just too busy at the moment to take my call. Her drowning was on my mind every day and upon waking from my nightmares to my screaming and night sweats. When those painful thoughts would try to move to the front of my mind on their own, I would quickly suppress them back to their place and put on what I called my "work face."

After a year of suppressing my mom's death, I didn't realize that each day throughout that year, those painful memories were automatically moving closer and closer, becoming more resistant to my suppressing power. Then the day happened that I thought could never happen to me because I was strong at not showing my feelings and not easily hurt or affected by people. My life circumstances had built up these impenetrable walls. I loved being alone because that's when I could let my guard down and feel safe. I thought that I could handle anything in my life until chronic depression hit me like a tsunami. I mean I didn't see it coming, nor did I know what had hit me, but I was no match for it. It knocked me about as low as I could go.

Why the Depression?

I was so embarrassed and ashamed to have to deal with depression. I asked God, "Why me? I am supposed to be the strong one in the family. After all, I was the Christian and the only one that had fallen apart."

God spoke to me later and told me why through the verse Romans 8:28.

> AND WE KNOW ALL THINGS WORK TOGETHER FOR GOOD TO THEM THAT LOVE GOD, TO THEM WHO ARE THE CALLED ACCORDING TO HIS PURPOSE. (Romans 8:28 King James Version)

We live in a corrupt world, so bad things will happen to us as Christians. But if we stay focused and obedient to God's ways, no matter the circumstances, as long as Christ is in our hearts, we will come out victorious. It is not all about us being happy in this life. It's about where we're going to spend eternity and working to take as many people to heaven as we can.

I know now that God allowed my depression to show me my sin of hatred and unforgiveness that I had for both my parents and my abusers. Although I loved Christ and tried to live my life for him daily, I was sinning and didn't even realize it. Here I was giving power to the dead to control me for giving them the victory over me. Oh, yes, I had told God many times that I forgave them and I also asked him to forgive me for my hatred. Through this depression I learned that I was only spitting words out. That I knew what to say, but it did not come from my heart, spirit, or soul. My anger, hate, and unforgiveness was very much alive. God knew it and needed to free me so his purpose could be fulfilled.

Depression had such a strong choke hold on me, I would cry when I woke up in the morning, and throughout the night, unable to sleep. I would try hard and tell myself that nothing was wrong with me; I just needed to shake out of this, never expecting that I could be depressed due to the death of my mother. This was just a mourning phase that would soon pass, but it was taking too long. I needed to get over this quickly because I needed to be a wife and a mother for my family.

As the depression deepened, I began to isolate myself from friends and family, hiding myself in closets so my husband and kids could not see me crying. The waterworks were so uncontrollable that I often found myself sitting in a parking lot, waiting for the crying to stop. It was hindering all areas of my life, including my eating, thinking, speaking, and driving. I became so embarrassed to be around people. Even their presence sent me into anxiety overload. I just did not want anyone to ask me why I was crying, because honestly, I did not know. I only came up with a lot of reasons why I should not be crying. I was not pregnant, no PMS nor menopause at the time. Happy marriage, family healthy, a good job, and a roof over our heads.

I was afraid people would think that I was ungrateful or a freak because that is actually how I felt. Smacking myself in the face felt like the right thing to do at the time. I was beginning to hate myself because I was no longer in control of my emotions. My husband, family, and friends began to see that I was avoiding them and encouraged me to get professional help. I was still in denial and I refused, assuring them that I was mourning my mom's death and that it would end soon and I would be fine. I promised my husband that if my attitude toward him and the kids changed for the worse, I would seek professional help for the sake of my marriage and parenting.

My anxiety started to increase, leveling off at 10 daily. The mental overload was very exhausting. I just wanted to run away. I could not take another "mommy" or house chore because I literally had nothing else to give. That was hard for my family and me because I'm usually a multitasker, like most women. I could not even do the basics. I actually had to wait and rely on my husband to get things done in and out of the home. Thank God for giving him the strength and the ability to get things done. He really stepped up to the plate.

I started having physical pain all over my body daily, both my heart and stomach. I was always feeling nauseous with no appetite. My work performance was affected due to my inability to focus. I even had memory loss more than normal for my age. That's when I went to see a psychiatrist, although reluctantly. Sitting in their office, far away from everyone else in a corner, I could not control the crying and I didn't want anyone to see me. The anxiety of waiting for my name to be called was so high that I was afraid if they did not call me soon, I was going to start screaming uncontrollably and be taken out on a stretcher to a psych ward. I was mentally tortured while sitting there.

When you are chronically depressed, you see things worse than they are, which sends your anxiety skyrocketing, losing your ability to reason and be rational. I prayed and prayed for God to calm me down and for them to hurry and call my name. I was thanking God when they finally called me to the back. This being my first time there, I did not know what to expect from the psychiatrist. To my surprise, there was no couch to lie on. I had already decided what I was going to tell him about my life, and it was very little. I sat with my arms crossed, guards up, giving only yes or no answers because I didn't want to hear the "D" word.

You see, in my mind, being diagnosed with chronic depression meant that I was following in my mother's footsteps, and that made me feel like a weak failure, crazy, and as if I was going to get addicted to psych meds. This is the very thing that I worked so hard not to become because I saw my mother suffer a lot. If I lived my life doing the opposite of her and my father, I would be happy. I planned on not telling the doctor about my mother's death or my childhood because surely he would say that I was depressed. I was sure that there was no way he was going to get it out of me.

I have to give a lot of credit to psychologists and psychiatrists for their expertise in the medical profession. I have to admit that even as a nurse, I felt like they were for crazy people who could not handle their problems. I am their number one fan. If they are good, they can get the most stubborn people to talk about those dark places in their life that no one likes revisiting. Why they like listening to everyone's problems and being dumped on like a trash can, I will never know. But I thank God for their gifts and calling. I think everyone should visit a therapist or counselor at least once, even if you are a Christian. You will be surprised at what is in you that you are unaware of, and whatever is in you that is not healthy needs to come out.

The professionalism and expertise of the psychiatrist that I saw caused me to open up, telling him more than I had planned to. My mouth was like a water fountain with words flowing out continuously until I could no longer get logical words out due to my crying. He told me I was chronically depressed, which to me sounded like a death sentence. He wanted me to start taking two different types of psych pills. I told him that I was afraid of taking those pills as I was never a person to take medicine. I would rather suffer from my illness, but most of all I feared getting addicted like my parents. I judged myself as now being crazy.

I felt like my life was going backwards. After all that living for Jesus, how could I be depressed? I must not be a true Christian. People started telling me that it was the devil playing mind games with me and that I needed to pray more. To get into God's word, so the devil would flee. Tell the devil he was a liar because I was not depressed. I did say it, but that time I was lying because depression was all over me. They told me not to claim depression, and trust me, I didn't. I would never claim such an illness. Depression claimed me.

I had many hands laid on me for prayer, prayer over the phone, books on prayer given to me. I was told that I just needed to snap out of it. This came from people that I knew loved me and would never intentionally hurt me, so I tried it all. I wanted out, but none of it worked; it just made me feel very ashamed to be around them. I felt like I failed God as a Christian because his word says in Isaiah 26:3:

> THOU WILT KEEP HIM IN PERFECT PEACE, WHOSE MIND IS STAYED ON THEE: BECAUSE HE TRUSTETH IN THEE.
> (Isaiah 26:3, King James Version)

I must not have been keeping my mind on him. I felt guilty for allowing myself to fall into depression, sinking into this big, dark hole like quicksand with no way out.

I know that it was the Christ in me, seeing my parents' addiction, and the love for my husband and kids that truly kept me from going down that road of drugs, alcohol, or suicide. I always saw suicide as a selfish act, but when you are in such a dark place, you have nothing to give. I'm talking emotionally depleted and you just want out, no matter the cost. In your delusional state of mind, you actually feel the opposite. You feel like you are relieving your family from their burden of you and your issues. I would

73

rather have my leg amputated, with no anesthesia or pain medication, than to ever be in that dark place again.

They are Forgiven

Through my asking God to help me forgive and love, yes, I said love, my abusers, God showed me some things that they may have gone through to cause them to do what they did, like their insecurities. Abusing others was their defense coping mechanism, having been abused themselves. Hurting people hurt people. God showed me that I could not judge my abusers because when I was of school age, I had hurt my family, friends, and schoolmates in the midst of my hurting. I again asked for forgiveness from those I had hurt in the past, from the bottom of my heart. No matter what my reason was, I did not have the right to hurt you. No one deserves to be treated that way.

Thank God for saving me. I am a new person now, as it says in 2 Corinthians 5:17:

THEREFORE IF ANY MAN BE IN CHRIST, HE IS A NEW CREATURE: OLD THINGS ARE PASSED AWAY; BEHOLD, ALL THINGS ARE BECOME NEW. (2 Corinthians 5:17)

My anger has been replaced with compassion and love, and my unforgiveness with genuine forgiveness from the heart. Although I am not really sure where my abusers will be eternally, I pray that God shows mercy toward them on Judgment Day and that he allows them to enter into his eternal glory. I can honestly say if I could stand in the gap for them, pleading to God on their behalf, I would. I never thought I would be in such a place of forgiveness.

I feel free and even more free as I've searched God's word to write this book. Wow! Look at me; I have been set free, just like in John 8:31-32:

> **THEN SAID JESUS TO THOSE JEWS WHICH BELIEVED ON HIM, IF YE CONTINUE IN MY WORD, THEN ARE YE MY DISCIPLES INDEED; AND YE SHALL KNOW THE TRUTH, AND THE TRUTH SHALL MAKE YOU FREE.**
> **(John 8:1-32, King James Version)**

Thank you, Lord, for lifting the burden of unforgiveness.

Where Were You God?

I often asked God to show me where he was during my abusive childhood. What did I do wrong to deserve this? I was blown away when he revealed his answer to me.

He sent me to some scriptures. One was Deuteronomy 7:6:

> FOR THOU ART AN HOLY PEOPLE UNTO THE LORD THY GOD: THE LORD THY GOD HATH CHOSEN THEE TO BE A SPECIAL PEOPLE UNTO HIMSELF, ABOVE ALL PEOPLE THAT ARE UPON THE FACE OF THE EARTH.
> (Deuteronomy 7:6, King James Version)

Wow, God made me feel like royalty. Talk about my self-esteem increasing. You mean you were there from my very foundation, down to the decision of both parents' alcohol and drug addictions?

He said, "I loved your parents, too and I needed you to help them, which you did. You see, my child, they were all a part of your testimony, so that I may get the glory as you go and tell of your story. The fact that you grew up in a house where there were no books, attended the worst elementary schools in the city, no high school or college graduates in your immediate family, all led to a very weak phonic foundation."

My grades were Ds and Fs all throughout elementary and middle school. I didn't have a reason to try because I was expected to fail, always being called a stupid #$$. Those words took root and I believed them; after all, they were coming from my authority figures. I always said that I hated to read, but I now know it was because I didn't understand what I was reading. For God to use me to write a book is a true representation of his word when he said in Romans 8:28:

> ## AND WE KNOW THAT ALL THINGS WORK TOGETHER FOR GOOD TO THEM THAT LOVE GOD, TO THEM WHO ARE CALLED ACCORDING TO HIS PURPOSE. (Romans 8:28, King James Version)

Although I feel like I lived with Lucifer in the flesh, going through persecution and abuse at a very early age, he could not tear this building down, nor subdue me.

Yes, my abusers were bigger than me, in the physical, but look who's my footstool. Because of them, I am being used in a big way by God for his kingdom. I may have scars on my back, like a field plowed by a farmer, like in Psalm 129:3. Furrows are long, narrow cuts farmers make in the dirt to plant seeds. The whole passage of Psalm 129:3-8 says:

79

Just like Israel, who were God's chosen people, faced persecution in their earlier days, yet never completely being destroyed. Or like Jesus, enduring unjust lashes from a whip on his back, punished to death for you and I. We need to come to God and his word when we are going through trials and feeling persecuted to find comfort. He promises in John 16:33 (King James Version):

> **THESE THINGS I HAVE SPOKEN UNTO YOU, THAT IN ME YE MIGHT HAVE PEACE. IN THE WORLD YE SHALL HAVE TRIBULATION: BUT BE OF GOOD CHEER; I HAVE OVERCOME THE WORLD." SO DON'T RUN FROM YOUR PROBLEMS, EXPECT THEM AND INSTEAD RUN TO GOD. YOU ARE PROMISED TO COME OUT ON TOP. ALLOW GOD TO USE YOUR SCARS AS STARS FOR THIS DYING WORLD TO SEE HOW GREAT AND MIGHTY HE IS.**
> **(John 16:33, King James Version)**

The Healing

"But ye are a chosen generation, a royal priesthood, an holy nation, a peculiar people, that ye should shew forth the praises of him who hath called you out of darkness into his marvelous light" (I Peter 2:9, King James Version).

To most people, being royalty means to be served by others, but in Christ we are to serve others, telling them all about what God has done, not about what we have accomplished in this life. The truth is the one thing that really counts is how our life is a representation of Christ, so that we may lead the lost and hurting people to him.

NOW THANKS BE UNTO GOD, WHICH ALWAYS CAUSETH US TO TRIUMPH IN CHRIST, AND MAKETH MANIFEST THE SAVIOR OF HIS KNOWLEDGE BY US IN EVERY PLACE. (2 Corinthians 2:14, King James Version)

Paul was thanking God for using him to minister to the Corinthians, even though he encountered difficulties. During these times back in Rome, people worshiped many different Gods. Whenever their God would come to their rescue during battle, there would be a procession of triumph and incense would be burned for their God. If you were a believer of that God, the aroma of the incense would smell like sweet victory. But if you did not believe in that God, it would be a foul, death-like smell.

I give God the praise and honor for rescuing me from my childhood hurts. He gave me the strength to overcome the burden of unforgiveness, and writing this book is my way of marching for him, burning an incense with the sweet aroma of victory, as I tell others my story for God's glory.

I love you, my brothers and sisters in Christ, and I pray that God shows you why your life had to take the path that it took. I pray that you will allow him to lift every burden and heal you from the flesh-eating disease of unforgiveness. I pray that you find deliverance and healing through this book as I have found writing it. May God give you the strength to tell your testimony so others may be saved, and remember you were chosen because he knew that you would come through. I will be praying for you.

Abuse

According to child abuse statistics created by http://www.childhelp.org/, an estimated 3 million reports of child abuse are reported each year. To learn the signs of child abuse and how you can help, please visit www.childwelfare.gov.

To learn more about how you can help victims of domestic violence and abuse please visit http://helpguide.org/ .

An estimated 19 million adult Americans are living with depression according to WebMD. ("Depression." *Side Effects of Untreated*. WedMD. Web. 10 Oct. 2014. <http://www.m.webmd.com /depression/guide/untreated-depression-effects? page=6>).

Depression is often judged by society as a sign of going crazy, weakness, having a negative attitude or not being close to God. This leads to feelings of guilt and embarrassment resulting in not seeking much needed medical treatment.

To learn the signs and symptoms of depression and how you can get help, or help someone else, please visit www.midwestcenter.com and talk with a medical provider. It may even save a life.

Journal

Abusers contaminate their victims like a disease. If left untreated, it continues to spread from person to person, causing emotional, physical, spiritual, and psychological death. Breaking these generational curses begins with getting what's in you out! Just like in the natural, what goes in must come out. So work your way through by writing in this journal section of the book and watch God begin your healing.

"Then they cried unto the LORD in their trouble, and he delivered them out of all their distresses." (Psalm 107:6, King James Version)

I love you and will be praying for your deliverance.

Write a letter to all who hurt you, explaining in detail all that you remember of the hurt.

_____

_____

_____

_____

_____

_____

_____

_____

_____

_____

_____

_____

_____

_____

_____

_____

_____

_____

_____

_____

_____

Now, pray, asking God to cast out all the hurt.

"He will turn again, he will have compassion upon us: he will subdue our iniquities: and thou wilt cast all their sins into the depths of the sea" (Micah 7:19).

_____

_____

_____

_____

_____

_____

_____

_____

_____

_____

_____

_____

_____

_____

_____

_____

Write a letter of forgiveness to all who hurt you, explaining why you forgive them even if they didn't ask for it.

_____

_____

_____

_____

_____

_____

_____

_____

_____

_____

_____

_____

_____

_____

_____

_____

_____

_____

"And when ye stand praying, forgive, if ye have ought against any: that your Father also which is in heaven may forgive your trespasses" (Mark 11:25, King James Version).

_____

_____

_____

_____

_____

_____

_____

_____

_____

_____

_____

_____

_____

_____

_____

_____

Pray, asking God to help you forgive.

Write a prayer asking God to save and heal all those who hurt you.

_____

_____

_____

_____

_____

_____

_____

_____

_____

_____

_____

_____

_____

_____

_____

_____

"Confess your faults one to another, and pray one for another, that ye may be healed. The effectual fervent prayer of a righteous man availeth much" (James 5:16, King James Version).

Pray and write, asking God to reveal his presence in the midst of your distress.

Write God's answer.

_____

_____

_____

_____

_____

_____

_____

_____

_____

_____

_____

_____

"And the LORD, he it is that doth go before thee: he will be with thee, he will not fail thee, neither forsake thee: fear not, neither be dismayed" (Deuteronomy 31:8, King James Version).

_____

_____

_____

_____

_____

_____

_____

_____

_____

_____

_____

_____

_____

_____

_____

_____

_____

_____

Ask God, "Why me, Lord?"

_____

_____

_____

_____

_____

_____

_____

_____

_____

_____

_____

_____

_____

_____

_____

_____

_____

_____

_____

"For I know the thoughts that I think toward you, saith the LORD, thoughts of peace, and not of evil, to give you an expected end" (Jeremiah 29:11).

_____

_____

_____

_____

_____

_____

_____

_____

_____

_____

_____

_____

_____

_____

_____

_____

_____

_____

_____

Write and date a letter to God asking, "Where do you want me to go from here?"

_____

_____

_____

_____

_____

_____

_____

_____

_____

_____

_____

_____

_____

_____

_____

_____

_____

_____

_____

_____

_____

_____

"I will instruct thee and teach thee in the way which thou shalt go: I will guide thee with mine eye" (Psalm 32:8, King James Version).

_____

_____

_____

_____

_____

_____

_____

_____

_____

_____

_____

_____

_____

_____

_____

_____

_____

_____

_____

Write how you think God can use your scars as stars for his glory.

_____

_____

_____

_____

_____

_____

_____

_____

_____

_____

_____

_____

_____

_____

"No matter how you were conceived to get into this world God still has a plan for you, like Ishmael although he was not the miracle baby for Abraham and Sarah. He was actually the result of Abraham and Sarah playing God, but in spite of his parents, God still blessed Ishmael to be the father over a great nation" (Genesis 17:20)

"Behold, I have refined thee, but not with silver, I have chosen thee in the furnace of affliction" (Isaiah 48:10, King James Version).

I know sometimes when we pray it feels like God is nowhere to be found or has forgotten us. I have learned in the midst of my waiting season that there is a good reason for the delays.

"And he spake a parable unto them to this end, that men ought always to pray, and not to faint;" (Luke 18:1, King James Version)

Pray over the scripture that is on the following pages and write what God speaks to you. Use the provided space to write down your response to the verses, how God may be using them to touch your life.

"Let us draw near with a true heart in full assurance of faith, having our hearts sprinkled from an evil conscience, and our bodies washed with pure water. Let us hold fast the profession of our faith without wavering; (for he is faithful that promised;)" (Hebrews 10:22-23, King James Version)

_____

_____

_____

_____

_____

_____

_____

_____

_____

_____

_____

_____

_____

_____

_____

_____

_____

"But thou, O man of God, flee these things; and follow after righteousness, godliness, faith, love, patience, meekness. Fight the good fight of faith, lay hold on eternal life, whereunto thou art also called, and hast professed a good profession before many witnesses" (1 Timothy 6:11-12, King James Version).

_____

_____

_____

_____

_____

_____

_____

_____

_____

_____

_____

_____

_____

_____

_____

_____

"Behold, his soul which is lifted up is not upright in him: but the just shall live by his faith" (Habakkuk 2:4, King James Version).

_____

_____

_____

_____

_____

_____

_____

_____

_____

_____

_____

_____

_____

_____

_____

_____

_____

"For verily I say unto you, That whosoever shall say unto this mountain, Be thou removed, and be thou cast into the sea; and shall not doubt in his heart, but shall believe that those things which he saith shall come to pass; he shall have whatsoever he saith" (Mark 11:23, King James Version).

_____

_____

_____

_____

_____

_____

_____

_____

_____

_____

_____

_____

_____

_____

_____

_____

_____

"For whatsoever is born of God overcometh the world: and this is the victory that overcometh the world, even our faith. Who is he that overcometh the world, but he that believeth that Jesus is the Son of God?" (1 John 5:4-5, King James Version)

_____

_____

_____

_____

_____

_____

_____

_____

_____

_____

_____

_____

_____

_____

_____

_____

"Nay, in all these things we are more than conquerors through him that loved us" (Romans 8:37, King James Version).

_____

_____

_____

_____

_____

_____

_____

_____

_____

_____

_____

_____

_____

_____

_____

_____

"For by wise counsel thou shalt make thy war: and in multitude of counsellors there is safety" (Proverbs 24:6, King James Version).

_____

_____

_____

_____

_____

_____

_____

_____

_____

_____

_____

_____

_____

_____

_____

_____

_____

_____

"Set your affection on things above, not on things on the earth" (Colossians 3:2, King James Version).

_____

_____

_____

_____

_____

_____

_____

_____

_____

_____

_____

_____

_____

_____

_____

_____

_____

_____

_____

_____

_____

_____

"But they that wait upon the Lord shall renew their strength; they shall mount up with wings as eagles; they shall run, and not be weary; and they shall walk, and not faint" (Isaiah 40:31, King James Version).

_____

_____

_____

_____

_____

_____

_____

_____

_____

_____

_____

_____

_____

_____

_____

_____

_____

"And if we know that he hear us, whatsoever we ask, we know that we have the petitions that we desired of him" (1 John 5:15, King James Version).

_____

_____

_____

_____

_____

_____

_____

_____

_____

_____

_____

_____

_____

_____

_____

_____

_____

_____

_____

"Therefore, my beloved brethren, be ye stedfast, unmoveable, always abounding in the work of the Lord, forasmuch as ye know that your labour is not in vain in the Lord" (1 Corinthians 15:58, King James Version).

_____

_____

_____

_____

_____

_____

_____

_____

_____

_____

_____

_____

_____

_____

_____

_____

_____

_____

"I love them that love me; and those that seek me early shall find me" (Proverbs 8:17, King James Version).

_____

_____

_____

_____

_____

_____

_____

_____

_____

_____

_____

_____

_____

_____

_____

_____

_____

_____

"Keep thy heart with all diligence; for out of it are the issues of life" (Proverbs 4:23, King James Version).

_____

_____

_____

_____

_____

_____

_____

_____

_____

_____

_____

_____

_____

_____

_____

_____

"Thine, O Lord, is the greatness, and the power, and the glory, and the victory, and the majesty: for all that is in the heaven and in the earth is thine; thine is the kingdom, O Lord , and thou art exalted as head above all"
(1 Chronicles 29:11, King James Version).

_____

_____

_____

_____

_____

_____

_____

_____

_____

_____

_____

_____

_____

_____

_____

_____

_____

_____

For **God** *so loved the world, that he gave his only begotten Son, that whosoever believeth in him should not perish, but have everlasting life.*

For God sent not his Son into the world to condemn the world; but that the world through him might be saved.

He that believeth on him is not condemned: but he that believeth not is condemned already, because he hath not believed in the name of the only begotten Son of God.

(John 3:16-18, King James Version)